Defying the Eye Chart

Defying the Eye Chart

Marilyn Jurich

Mayapple Press 2008

Published by   Mayapple Press
                 408 N. Lincoln St.
                 Bay City, MI 48708
                 www.mayapplepress.com

ISBN 978-0932412-577

ACKNOWLEDGMENTS

"Even Death Is Uncertain Without the Proper Forms": *Femspec*
"The Immutable": *Do Not Give Me Things Unbroken*
"Reading the Eye Chart," "The Seamstress of Flowers, After Grimms' 'The Six Swans,'" "Tachonic Toss #1, for Frank Capra," and "Threat": *Uncommonplaces: Poems of the Fantastic* (Mayapple Press, 2000)
"Minding the Trickster": *Trickster's Way*
"Scourge for Accidental Voyeurs": *Venture*
"Mozart's Sister": *Ariel, A Review of International English Literature*

Photo of Marilyn Jurich by William Walcott. Sculpture, "Head of a Woman" by Betty Z. Kerman.

Cover and book designed by Judith Kerman. Book typeset by Amee Schmidt with text and titles in Adobe Caslon Pro.

Contents

1. Anatomies of Light and Dark

2. Daring to Look at the Sacred

3. Reflections of Past Lives

4. Perspectives of Gender: Sister & Brother

1. Anatomies of Light and Dark

Reading the Eye Chart

Trick the gullible eye—
Lines stick out their tongues, diagonals curve.
Vipers hiss from Druid stones under a white sky.
Advancing shadows dance or die,
trick the gullible eye—
embracing fitful ghosts, longing to tie
circle-line to sense before they swerve,
trick the gullible eye.
Lines stick out their tongues, diagonals curve.

This is the alphabet of ferns
singing between the passages of wind.
Dream language of the lover who yearns
for echoing syllable as he gently turns.
This is the alphabet of ferns.
Whoever learns to see one code, design… listen and rescind.
This is the alphabet of ferns
singing between the passages of wind.

Unraveling my soul by what I see
you count how close I come to hold desire,
gauge my level of normality
according to whether I call the shrinking letter E,
unraveling my soul by what I see,
convinced the eye uncovers mystery—
omphalos to everything we can aspire.
Unraveling my soul by what I see,
you count how close I come to hold desire.

Macula

Experience in Macular Degeneration: A Progress Report

1.

Flawed daisy wants a corolla. Bracts
entwine the flowers as minuets
undanced to notes on the brink of sound.
These ghosts are not to be exorcised.

In June the radiant beams of dawn—
carillon bells in their hymn to day—
surprise our bodies half courting dream,
content in landscape, amorphous, mute.
These ghosts are not to be exorcised.

Pretend accordion folds expand,
contract.   No player determine how
or why. The stairways descend. I fall.
These ghosts are not to be exorcised.

The rules of facing are only two:
Imagine. Trick. In a smile the O-
pen mouth, each lip in a play of tag.
Or nod aslant at the ear unhinged.
These ghosts are not to be exorcised.

A kite is flying inside the moon.
These ghosts are not to be exorcised.
I see-saw down as the sun comes up
and shadows rise as the *ghosts* of day.

2.

Low tide, confetti of seaweed, shells—
the snail that burrows in silence, blind
to children wriggling in wag-tail waves.
O turn away from the flounder's eye.

The tails of peacocks fan eyes that flame.
In flames the eyes are an orange-red
that slant like thread from a needle's eye.
Don't turn away from the flounder's eye.

Potato eyes have a pink-white bud—
If eyes could bud… only Argus knows.
And some have eyes at the back of heads.
O turn away from the flounder's eye.

"Beware the eye of the storm," you say.
"The evil eye can be lured by charms.
The eye will hear if a man rings true.
Don't turn away from the flounder's eye."

I fish for eyes in the seas of glass.
O turn away from the flounder's eye
that pierce the soul with the spear of dread,
of loss.   My eyes *will not turn* to weep.

3.

Horizons tunnel and caverns dome.
Green mist dissolves in a silver sky.
The car wheels swim to the motor's drone.
Things fall apart when the center fails.

Without their faces all clocks are stilled
and skin looks young in unfacing glass.
Through shifting contours I choose a mask,
invent a mouth with salacious lips.
Things fall apart when the center fails.

"A doughnut life is a sticky fraud"—
your joke. I scowl, "It's a reeking hole
more foul than sweet, the circumference dim."
Now you develop the metaphor.
Things fall apart when the center fails.

If eyes plays tricks, you can trick your eyes.
Things fall apart when the center fails
unless you make the corolla rise
from eyes which center on things that last.

Resisting Blindness

        No.
              Blindness for Wisdom
              I will not trade.
              Neither believe
              the wise see better, further,
              inevitably preserve the world.

The Eye of Day—daisy, cat's eye, cunning jewel.
Fish eyes glisten from ice chips
through window glass;
bulging stares like boxing gloves assault
in sightless irony.   Scorpions are sightless.
How can they see?   *No eyes.*
October the Scorpion, poor creature
who plodding on enchanted leaves—
purple, scarlet, golden—stays himself
blind to where he's been.

October, my birth month, glorious and sad.

        Shall I be Chlamydomonas
        floating toward the light,
        fibrils urged by eye spots to the dawn,
        groping for that eye of day?
        Horus blinded.   One-eyed Horus was too gentle.
        Cyclops for all his fierceness, simple.
        Eyes seeking death are strongest,
        compound design:
        countless tunneled chambers, the switches tapped,
        devise the sudden execution of a prey.

        I should have been a praying mantis
        keen for victims playing righteous.
        Myopes cannot play, I'm told.
        Too eager, searching for the Holy Ghost,
        they cannot climb the trees of heaven.
        Intent on understanding every leaf
        they stop and stumble,
        never to sight mountains.

Ease downwards then
toward earth, messy and sublime;
the bottom of the tree trunk carved—
letters, numbers—
Trace with steady fingers, shape
a multi-layered people
talking, making, leaping
as vast filaments   extending.

Swirl yesterday to sunset
trusting distance and desire,
the elegant design.

      … a certain Chinese landscape,
      plum blossoms at beginning day,
      persuades me of a special vision.
      Dew so infinitesimal, glistens;
      one branch lingers as in longing.
      A crescent form—bird wing or leaf—
      floats in one corner of the scroll…

Ghosts created by imperfect eyes
lift us into others' memory
connecting who we are.

Even death is uncertain
without the proper forms

His hand circles on the desk, delves underneath
and raises, as if it were a crucible,
a sheet of paper, this streaked with light
glowing from one cuff-link,
a large gold sphere I have to dodge.
His mouth is sinuous inside his beard,
conjuring up sounds not visible
while his eyes are everywhere
vaulting across the table to ignite my brain.

He plays his voice, fondling each stop.
"Your own eyes—that trouble—yes, no doubt—
after looking at the benefits of course—
you'll want to donate—a *mitzvah*—
your mother's eyes, her corneas, you know."

Your darkness, Mother, would be another's
light. Will I have your blessing? God's?
Oh shame of empty sockets
and you in your new gray suit!
Do they fill the eyes with stones?
Paint ebony eyes on linen?

My words are fragments caught inside a vise.
Chayim—life—still grow from her eyes?
Can God refuse a miracle?
Such questions do not serve expedience,
and he only waits. "I need to feel my way,"
I tell him.   I am confused, ashamed.

What do the rabbis tell us? What should
a daughter know? What sisters?

I look to aunts all grim against one wall.
"Never," my Aunt Rena shrieks, eyes
angry, terrified. "No one robs the grave.
Pluck out her eyes, you'll have God's curse."

"God means to heal, will bend the law," I say.
I long for understanding, trust. Long for
sanction or denial, some answer out of love.

The two other aunts are silence, stare.
Rena claws her chest.   Three Liliths
who look for demons in another's soul.

Discs on his cuffs trigger V-shaped light.
From cradled palms he fans out glossy nails,
retracts two fingers he raises to a steeple.
"We have to know—prepare the corpse."
He speaks from half-closed eyes.

And does the soul need eyes?   the other self?
Do I barter eyes for my design?
The child sacrifices the parent out of
principle.   Love—it is merely camouflage?
Can she want her eyes in a stranger's face,
she who flinched from touch,
wiped away my kiss?

Stranger that you were, Mother, be my
child.   Let me find your way.   Join me
*in the **kaddish** prayer.*

Rena whispers, "You'd give away her eyes,
she who gave you sight?   You saw
her suffer. You'd have her suffer more?"

Tattooed with punctures, pin-holes,
body a game for darts.   A Kewpie doll
swung on a stick for "tries." Poor clown
smiles at doctors, nurses, putting on
a face.   Innocent playing at hope.

Sarah, the oldest, turns to Rena,
voice ashen, low. "You never saw her suffer.
Preferred comfort and good times.
How the blind speak of seeing!"

Aunt Lil, complacent and pretty, studies
her gold and diamond watch.

Numbers on a watch I strained to see—
*how many years?   I remembered **her** gold watch,*
my mother's birthday gift.   Twenty-one,
first year away from home. It was my special candle
                              and my crown.

Her eyes... another gift?   Hers?   Mine?

Eyes flickering, hands teasing at his beard,
he says to all of us, to me. "These eyes—
too old for anyone to see.   Used as
specimens for students to dissect."

"Samson lost vision, not his wits,"
I say, "and pillars take on many shapes."
He slides the form beneath his hands.

On the funeral day he comes up close,
smoothes his arm against my own—
that line of smile inside his beard.
"You're quite decided what the family wants?
One last goodbye face to face gives closure,
most agree."

"The coffin stays closed."
I face him to avert sly argument,
to prove a strength I cannot know.
Mother, no one sees you, only God

who gives your eyes His light—your eyes
inviolate as your soul.

I am anxious, though.
Who can be so certain?

Does he snare corneas in his cuff-links,
sell eyes as souvenirs,
or wear the cobra eye,
the proper form of power
to rule regions of sun-light,
to rule regions of the dark?

Tears—my tears—efface such power,
fuse image, sound to memory—
another landscape.
I hear fragments, then the whole refrain.
"Keyn eyn hore, sheyne madele."

Neighbors smile at me, a child of four,
at Mother who holds my hand.
"Mayn feygele," she looks at them,
turns her eyes to me.
She is happy and proud.

Several Yiddish terms are used in the poem. These are discussed in the order in which they appear.

Mitzvah signifies a moral act that serves God's will; an obligation or good deed offered with free will and out of loving spirit.

Kaddish is the prayer which closes all other prayers recited in the synagogue and the one prayer which is related to mourners. In fact, it is alluded to as "the mourner's prayer." Glorifying God's name and expressing the hope for peace, the prayer is an affirmation of faith in the establishment of God's kingdom. The mourner recites the prayer to recount the virtues of the dead and to pledge devotion to Judaic principles. A belief also exists that by praising God in the *Kaddish* prayer, the mourner will assist the soul of the dead to enjoy a lasting peace.

Keyn eyn hore is used as a charm to ward of the evil eye and is particularly invoked when a person remarks on the merits or good fortune of him/herself or others closely related. The fear is that in commending oneself or another, an individual may offend the gods (or spirits) by rousing them to jealousy or anger. Such *hubris*, it is felt, rarely goes unpunished.

Sheyne madele means "beautiful" or "pretty little girl".

Mayn feygele is a term of endearment that means "little bird" or "dear little girl" or, most likely, can mean both simultaneously.

Eye Contact, Madonnas, and Culture-shock

1 -   The wandering eyes that worry, calculate,
      watch for something that you fail to bring—
      you, intent and passionate, carrying eyes
      in hand, panting flowers just unhinged and
      breathless for another's care.
      Your eyes are kneecaps waiting to kneel
      to displaced icons. You start a prayer
      even as orbs accelerate and disappear
      like tail-lights on an empty street.

2 -   In Italy *"Come stai"*—eyes speak to yours
      no matter how you stutter, turn away
      timid, surprised, needing *giocare - giacare*
      (role-playing, lies), scared of who you are.
      Benevolent, their eyes are haloed arrows that
      hold you crucified—the tree
      of sinners and madonnas, motor-cycling
      dads. Punished by acceptance, your eyes turn to
      olives—melt with heat, resist all slants.

3 -   Svengali holds eyes like puppies on a leash,
      whips them to strike or slaver loyalty
      according to his whim. How, if
      "eyes know a lie"—my mother used to say—
      would the soul comply?
      Donne knew and lovers know: "Thread" eyes
      "upon one double string"—a single soul
      refined through ecstasy. The Sexual Divine.
      Who will mingle eyes in transformed blood?

4 -   I research eyes, too frequent witness of madonnas
      who look past their bambini, not that Jesus
      obliges. I am lonely for eyes.   Yes, di Paciano
      paints mother and child, eyes meeting—
      archangels and saints look at them and smile.
      The two certainly attractive, poised
      on their starry throne. Robes threaded with gold
      match gold haloes. The eyes are dim,
      share denial which stretches past the fresco.

5 -   Do virgins want such motherhood?
       Look at Ghirlandio's red-haired girl
       as she fingers her baby's thigh, plump folds
       that offend the delicacies of white lace.
       The baby looks up to an abstract gaze.
       Though Christ can be a problem—brazen!
       See Ferrucci's baby struts his unsheathed
       penis—lucent against Mother's robe. His eyes
       want only acclaim—"See these grapes."

6 -   Raphael's babies tease their mothers' shawls,
       caress their sunburnt neck. Even so,
       these bosomy matrons are serenely blank.
       Earlier madonnas (see Fra Angelico's)
       swallow their infants with their eyes.
       Reverent, taste their God.

       And God—the vacant eye between clouds.
       How do we meet eye to eye?   Look—
       in Perugia all of us are children climbing hills.

Oedipus Visits the Ophthalmologist

What retina remains
to see, hook light to brain....
We'll soon know.   Lift up your head,
don't move now.
      King Oedipus, keep the eyes straight.

You pierced the sclera—the white—
pretty deep. The cornea scarred
as any Sphinx's riddle,
and the aqueous leaks.
      We'll need a cell count to assess.

Keep your head erect.   Oh where is
Royal Blood, the Crown of Thebes?
How to complete the angiogram,
such shuddering and moaning?
      Nurse, inject the Valium.

The vitreous seeps like jellied broth.
Yet, not too bad considering the gash,
twin naveled wounds, strange design
and cunning holes to heal.
      Here, record the millimeters, Nurse.

Oedipus, let's talk, bottom
line. Man to man. You crave
Phoebus, long to see your daughters—
sisters, are they?—Antigone, Ismene,
      nubile as crushed grapes.

Can I restore your vision,
sight—what you want to know and fear...?
"Wear malachite against the evil eye,"
every slave believes.
      For you, though, that eye coils in the gut.

No cover-up can hide the reason
you chose blindness. Thebes still aghast.
Let's rehearse the scene, how you pierced
the clasps through your eyeballs.
      Successor to Cadmus, calm your groans.

These weapons, clasps of brooches,
engraved with olive branch and owl,
you tore from Queen Jocasta's gown
the wife-mother dangling
          inside her seductive noose.

          O cover your face, Oedipus,
Jocasta's will not fade. Her skin blotched
and grey, eyes gaping,
as if struck with gorgon fangs.
          Truth brings light—stop whimmering.

          Tyrannous, you who shouted "Truth, truth,"
you could have stopped the prophet's mouth.
Teiresias like you blinded, amuck
with testosterone.
          Yet, to see the shimmering Athena naked!

          Confess, Thebes, how was it
to look at Jocasta, mother-wife?
Did you slaver on her womb?
Recall the amniotic
          thrill? Tease of placental swirl?

          Confess how sweet her nipples tasted,
gorging on her ambrosial milk,
with penis toward bursting. You lie
under one plump breast,
          your infant sucks the other.

          "Oedipus ground up his father's corpse
and shaped him into candied balls,"
the children sing. Call the candies
"Laius Heads." So sweet.
          Rage, Sovereign, you'll hemorrhage once again.

          So privileged and you still complain.
Born twice each time your twisting root
plunged into her, she rising fruit
and flower. Twice yours in granting
          immortality. How can you groan?

        Ah, fortunate! Who would exchange
the many eyes of Argus for memories
such as yours? And you're still
the people's hero. "Blame," they say,
"the Oracle of Delphi for such lust."

Of course, the tears won't flow.
Torn muscles cannot squeeze what may,
otherwise, be forced. We'll say
the Gods weep for *you*—or one, at least—
Cronus who debauched his sister, Rhea.

The angiogram shows no retina intact.
Well, vision would only be revenge.   Right?

                              Hang in there, King.

Unveiling of my Father

*"The rock, His work is perfect,
for all His Ways are judgment..."*
—Recitation at graveside

Sam left in steerage   died
into this ghetto,
tenements of stone,
teeth staring through grass sockets.

A glaring sky   empty branches.
Graphite tracings echo
names we seek to call and cannot
frame.

The living come, names raised high
in leather boots, hand-stitched in fine
lapels.   Arranging scarves, fur boas,
they fondle memory.

Lips take on a doleful contour
before the mouths resume
bored acrobatics of
the afternoon.

The stone calls them
and the veil,
not his laughter
spurting from the earth.

Pebbles topple from the monument,
fall onto the hard earth.
A few only
scatter on his grave.

"O Lord, what is man
that you regard him—
You knew this man, hard-working,
honest, loved—"

God's Faker ripples through
the rabbi's beard.
Time smiles gold from wrists
flickering with impatience.

The designated fingers move—
those of "male kindred closest
to deceased." Sam's daughter watches
the flawless ritual of hand.

Sam's brother persuades the cloth
to glide, each fold a grace note
as it falls away in perfect time
until the stone is bare...

The sun opens   names that know us
cut across the sky
splintering the blue, streaking
fallen branches, wintry rubble.

Relatives touch stone and letter, approve
the date   saunter toward each separate car.
One cousin grasps a bush, plucks berries.
Dark orange stains the path.

My father lightly rubs bruised fruits
inside one palm,
sits upon the earth and
grieves for me.

2. Daring to Look at the Sacred

Prayer Addict

> "*The obligation to recite Kaddish is placed upon the son,
> not upon the daughter. [Yet the daughter is encouraged]
> to respond fervently with the 'amen'...*"
> —Maurice Lamm,
> *The Jewish Way in Death and Mourning*

> ...*prayer as a means to effect a private end, is theft and
> meanness.*"
> —*Ralph Waldo Emerson, "Self-Reliance"*

Lottery of amens—"Amen, amen" once again
till wish turns prophecy, and year after year
the child lies awake and works in the dark.
The more "amens," I thought, God would be
moved. Like fingering piano keys till
the passage moves itself.

"...*birchasa v'shirasa,*" the upper teeth strike
the lower lip for "v," will not withdraw for "sh"—
smooth flow restrained. Legato broken.
I would be perfect without pause, not for God,
for her.

"*Hu ya 'aseh shalom*"—A's breathe like petals
inside a candle flame. "...may He make peace,"
I translate for us both. We listen in my closet,
cinema of memory, synagogue—
holy relics hid between and under...

Red cotton blouse with bursts of polka dots
she wore to cheer herself... yes darting
to the table with a store-bought cake. "Not
like mine, so light! Remember..." Showing
us her "latest book," a celebrity's life
she had deserved, missed.

Oh, elegant profile surrounded by roses,
hair coiffed in tiers, she wears a pendant and
earrings—diamonds flash against dark

amber.   That cameo bought
on Delancey one day—how many paychecks?

In the same jewelry tray, four prongs of gold
equidistant on a curve—
her bridge of poor teeth, one incisor, four molars.
Biting and tearing always too hard. Swallowing—
not easy. I find her spittle in my mouth
when I try these sounds.   Begin.

"B'olomo deev'ro chir'usai"—"In this world which He
has created in accordance with his Will…"
And where is your will, brother?   Your soul?
My brother, the scholar, punctual always,
mouths Kaddish only on the prescribed Yahr-
zeit…. He follows the Law and God waves okay.

The authorities nod, and, of course, *she* approves,
cries out in joy—joy through the year—
while I grieve each day—matins and vespers—
that her number came up   and none of us
won. What's left—only this stupid truth of prayer.
"Amen, amen…"   and it never works.

Ceres Ponders "Ratto Di Proserpina"
Galleria Borghese, Roma, 1998

Like a vise, Hades' fingers clamp Persephone's thigh.
Listen, Persephone's silent gasp   mouth toppled like
a fallen vase. Tears spill slant across one cheek,
                    cling as suspended petals.

Bud of woman, destined to bleed before she flowers darkly.

Hades is all muscled light, a jet stream of decisive ripples—
                    shoulder, arm, buttock, leg—
the twisting Gracilis, Sartorius bending.
Energy so massed, it plunges out of the marble.

Persephone in stasis   denying the lushness of her
smooth-skinned body, the fruit of buttock, breast and
belly, the white Carrara curves forcibly disturbed.   Frantic
angles—left knee clenched against right leg, the feeble lock.
Arms flinging in defense, the left thrusts at her rapist's
crown. The right hand climbs, seeks wings. Fingers
                    spread as chasms of air.

And here beside me is my daughter, sleeveless tee shirt
framing a soft neck, her arms more powerful than Koré's,
          Persephone's name as "Maiden."
I see the little hills that form my daughter's biceps.
          My daughter's skirt is circled with red flowers,
          and I wonder about the hidden layers,
          the precious folds I used to wash and talcum,
          diapering the whole.   I wonder about "the friend"
          who is not "boyfriend" in the gallery two rooms
          down. He is tall and smart and regularly smiles.

          My daughter does not smile, circling Hades.

She notes his beard of ringlets. Persephone's torn robe
is draped across his penis. Her left leg seals the cloth
till Cerberus, at Persephone's feet, will upset her
balance.   My daughter, I think, is streetwise, wiser than
          I was—or am. Yet, she is tender, becomes
          Orpheus to anyone's claim of Eurydice.

Persephone's mother was Ceres, right?" my daughter
asks the question. "Yes," I reply, "Ceres, goddess of
                    fertility, goddess of the grain."
            and I want to protect this seed leaf,
        want to make for her Pygmalion, the perfect man.

    I pull the strap of t-shirt over the insistent
    white strap of her bra   mean to pull her clear
from the Borghese, the summer decadence of Rome.
        Instead, I say, "Has your friend been here, looked at
                    this Bernini sculpture?"

Mother and daughter bring the friend to look.
    Surround him like silks of corn. Are still.
Nothing hovers or trembles, not sky or earth.

I do not know what my daughter thinks or feels.

    I think eight months too long in Hades.

Reversals

Hairs, leaves of weeping willows, grow for having lived.
The nails ascend to gothic heights, horns to scare the devil.
How the dead pretend! The smiling skeleton cancels time
for priests and scholars and thee. Come-hither bones emit
salacious luster. Temporal lobes, like raffish stars, revel
in our gaze, taunt our fears. What if some lever
in our brains dislodged Paradise, the Adam-Eve
debacle, instead pulled down *ersatz* Adam, *nouveau* Eve,
each on earth in separate times and relishing the sleep
called life—its bosomy fruit, lissome air, the peals
of birdsong, floating lilies, frog ooze in mud,
the snake flicking his curious tongue.   Nothing dumb,
obscene. Even God posits no trap.

Alas, who can be born (clone, messiah?) with man and woman
                    a-part—
in fact, preferring different eras.   Both baffled sore
in the other's presence and bored with Eden's Eros.
They want to grow tangerines, not apples, rock
the tree for the other "fruit," find the core
to how velocity determines mass. "What is rain?"
each wonders. "Light?" Both know the perils of "near"—
each body absorbed in the other's will. They feel
knowledge dissolves with flesh, truth turning to a fig leaf,
the source of real despair. Yet, each muses... *Another eye*
like ours, another foot with toes, a belly's eye
called "navel." Ah centuries collapse. Adam and Eve meet,
decide they are a team,

forget. Explore each other's flesh.   Deliver Evil
in   Cain, first killer and technician. "How to live
with death" becomes their only question. "Lease
Paradise to angels," Eve is bitter. "Seal
the gates," cries Adam. "A tainted land—seeps raw
garbage. Fangs, venom, adrenaline, the metals of war."
Both man and woman nod, "Love is a trap."
The sight of Abel's grave determines they must part.
Yet, neither moves. Each feels a lack
in that vacancy of love, a tender call

to save what Abel meant for the earth—to reach beyond death into a different knowledge. Cheer another world. Solemn, still wavering, they say "Yes. Yes."

Meditation of Perseus Before the Cave of Medusa

*"...Polydectes sent [Perseus] to attempt the conquest of
Medusa, a terrible monster who had laid waste to the
country."*
—*Bulfinch's Mythology*

Look too much—be careful.
Think of Oedipus and subways
where the casual glance puts your life on hold.
Orpheus lost his wife
for a glimmer of assurance,
poor Eurydice dragged back to Hades.

Worse than death is turning
into stone. Lot's wife, you know,
turned pillar, became her own grave site
(though salt has a small half-life).
Don't tell me rocks are awesome, sacred—
druid menhirs, mounts for saviors, gods.

Consider all the downside—
Mount Helena, Pompei, the flesh
turned to ash. Caucasus—ice-daggery
peaks sawed through Prometheus'
side as he struggled in his chains.
"Sinners" crushed by stones, witches drowned.

Jehovah, Zeus, my father,
inscribe their power in rock,
and all through time
Sisyphus heaves and pants.

I will not be coward, must face
the Gorgon— sense her spiky breath,
the terror of her ringlets,
those seething hydras, the coiling of her hips,
and streaked with blood and magma,
her granite eyes.

No mirror will I use to snare the image
to my sword. She can keep
her head and I am victor,
though stone—a sea green beryl, quartz
that ticks, stalagmites in the creatured
caves of Lascaux.

I would be house to barnacles and snails,
seat for lovers to embrace,
nursery for lichens.
I can be limestone in the cliffs of Mallam
freeing water into streams,
a flowing rock of water.

Medusa, calm your anger, grief. Perseus comes
to change life to life: granite into flesh
or flesh to rock.   Look.
Look into my face.

Minding the Trickster

He/she makes me angry—this fellow/gal and how
everyone winks an eye, turns his/her butt.
Tongues "tsse, tsse—too bad." Grins, the go-ahead
to turn everything around, no matter that the elevator tilts
sideways and we're pelted with doo-doo pooping through
a shaft (open, thanks to Legba, renegade, who never leaves
off punishing his mother, Mawu).
>   Don't call me "stick-in-the-mud"
>   for wanting a safe ride.
>   My jacket sloshed—and who's to pay?

Believe me, I understand "play." Applaud the child prodigy
of theft. Of course, it was a game.   Apollo, God of Sober
Thought, called off his grudge, won over by the lyre.
Poor tortoise. Robbed of his carapace, he was anyone's
quick meal, and Coyote—the same who sends his anus out
to hunt and farts between his teeth—stumbled into turtle
meat. So much for turtle holding up the world.
>   I tell you we are falling,
>   falling in whatever… worse than
>   the beginning.   Hermes in every mall.

Our benefactors? Forget it. Prometheus, misguided fool…
Recall "the road to sin is paved with good intentions."
Our hero began that trip.   Maybe Zeus knew better
than to give his children matches, land mines, and the whole
shebang. That blustering lecher knew the blazing groin,
how politicians ejaculate loaded missiles
to hide ballistic lust.

Now I like a laugh like anyone—I just don't get the joke.
Most tricks make me sick. Jael nailing the tent peg
into Sisera's head—funny to Yahweh? Save me
from such gods. For divine comedy, turn elsewhere. Maybe
Isis—vagina panting to an absent penis.   Pure Gothic,
Osiris resurrected, all except for *that*.   As for Circe
changing Odysseus' men to pigs?   Pure metaphor!

Trickster thrives on muck to get ahead. Clap, clap!
Wakdjunkaga takes a bow after gorging on—say blood-

red wine. Lives better than my uncle, sign-painter, who
couldn't read signs, worked over-time. Wife… not one child
with his DNA. Died young. "Too honest for his own good,"
Dad said, Dad who wore one suit for years and spotless.

       My mother specialized in cleanliness
       and shame, scrubbed my hair with tar
       soap. "Don't trust or try. Seeds fail."

Schlemiel, I flounder on piano keys, stay fixed
on rims of bottles, jars, I cannot turn.
Eyes fasten on a donkey's tail not there.
Blindfolded naturally.   Never any prize.
Couldn't snatch it no matter what.   Clumsy, scared of
rules and soft for tears.   Everyone pretends he/she
entitled. Everyone has something up that sleeve.

       I wear my father's suit, cuffs frayed. My scalp
       prickles—too dry. I wait for seed leaves,
       for Krishna and the Gopis.

       Hermes, sweet child, are you listening?

3. Reflections of Past Lives

Sidewalk Astronaut

Absolute unlife of August afternoons,
steaming trolley tracks   no car in sight,
not one drunk sprawled in a doorway
somewhere in Manhattan 1946
when for want of any one or thing
to do, she tossed balloons
onto her father's awning—balloon
after balloon—and who unmindful
of the self,   the object,
allowing each one to slide into her hands
or else to fumble and escape
without a grief,
she breathing another one to life,
blowing that droop of skin to swelling
and plugging that mouth-hole with a knot,
inevitable descent or slow
elopement
from that striped covering which shaded
the window of her father's store—
where everything was as she always
knew,
intervals of crayons plucked from boxes,
tilting rows of pens and notebooks
spread to show the lined or unlined page,
greeting cards according to the seasons—
and where after hours heavy zig-zag grids
pressed against the glass
splintering familiar shapes into a common-
place of irrational design
and she saw her life a series of
balloons   and listless days,
a routine of labeled items no one
cared about
that had to be protected
and she was still too little
to remember Sisyphus who, after all,
pushed the rock uphill
laughing
because the gods were scared.

25 Lines for Ascending and Descending Keys

She eight years old (was it I?)   watches me play.
I sixty odd (was it she?)   am watching her watching.
I make a mistake.
It was her (my) mistake.
We are both—double cacophony—mistaken
and laugh.   Neither has improved
this week or the last.
We hope next week (in the future and the past)
to win the Chopin Prize.

The eight-year old rises, sticks out her tongue.
I   (the she who used to be) refuse this mockery,
defeat—begin to practice "holds."
I taunt, "I'm better than what you could become"
and continue with *sforzando* finger-breaking chords
when, drat, my finger strikes F# instead of E.

"You'd be much better now if you'd listened
all those years, not closed your ears on me."

I answer, "The nerve! It was yourself that held me back."
"You were always childish," she replies. "Besides,
don't try your one-up-womanship on me."

"Okay" (I am mature). "Let's find the music, each one
listening to the other."   "Let's begin," she says.

Pushing back each pigtail, she plumps onto the bench,
joins me at the keyboard. We play a "Contra Dance" by
Beethoven   our duet in perfect time.

The Fast

Yom Kippur, New York, 1945

Two days a year my father closed the store
and on this, the highest of holy holidays
he slept past five.   How early do I glimpse
the lined up prayer book, tallith, yarmulke
beside the velvet case with Hebrew letters—
flags of God.   Three fingers dance a signal
before my lifting eyes. I nod and smile,
and skipping into my waiting dress, the opening
day, I see each bud of sunlight grow
into a secret. The dark blue suit immaculate
and formal charges my father with mystery.
He seems to step through air.   A glorious
hush.   We turn the knob… listen.   A distant
shuffling, my mother's sleep. We seal the door.

Tart blueness of October sky—the river
echoes in a gold staccato. We climb the hill
to Broadway clean and calm before the scrambling
bodies, cartons, dollies wheeled off trucks,
the clanking gates wrenched apart from store fronts,
eiyeeyes of pigeons scudding underfoot,
and rows of busses spewing. We breathe are blessed,
our feet rhyming to the crunch of leaves,
legs rising in duet like slides of trombones,
past Woolworth's, Yanow's grocery, the synagogue.
We smuggle into Bickfords, flesh tingling with
adventure, warmed by perky fragrances,
the fine edginess of bustle, easy clatter
of trays. I sit and watch my father eat.

A dome of pancakes braceleted in eggs,
toast radiant with butter, swirled in jam,
my father's grandest breakfast of the year
which God, I know, is sharing and enjoys—
the maple syrup running wild.   And I
looked on, not tempted, fat as sin and starved
for praise, desiring magic and reward, a prayer

to savor in my mouth.   "The syrup's fake
just like forgiveness," my father rose, flung out one arm
to embody all of Bickfords—maybe even God,
the dead in my mother's dreams, appearing to her now.
"The dead seek your forgiveness," said the rabbi....
On Broadway I drag my feet   feel empty.
Once inside the temple, my father and I will part.

Friday Nights and After

Jazz Piece for Aunt R—

As close as my idea of wild she came
in her black dress, thick ankles, blazing
lipstick, sizzling laughter.   She came and was
the wonder of her nose, prow jutting forward, forward,
pushed always to surprise—the nonsense of
her day selling clothes at Ohrbach's—who made
a good buy, how she argued with the manager,
"lump head," and had, today, found me—me, nine and fat as
a stuffed derma—something that would fit, the brown jumper
that I'd wear straight through grade school
to feel thin.

Aunt R was thin, "skinny as a rail, a string bean,"
thin as the spaghetti strands she'd wind around
her spoon when at Alfredo's—joy, she took me out,
really "out," downtown—and so many colored lights
there at Alfredo's and us
joking at the counter, my loops uncurling from my fork
quivering like Bing Crosby's croon, and Aunt R singing too,
singing above her platter and Alfredo looping arias
around her tunes while dishing out spumoni
and the rubber bands loosened from my braids, waves of
hair unwinding.

Fridays, on my mother's kitchen table
bowls of cabbage soup.   One by one Aunt R tossed out
raisins and for the umpteenth time scolded,
"Es, you know for me these are wrinkled bugs, *dreck*."
The mess of raisins nothing compared to bones,
fish bones sucked dry from smelts and cod.
Any bones she relished, fish bones most,
some so small you wondered how they wouldn't
tangle down her throat with chunks of challah,
rye bread she'd stuff down with her tea.   You prized
that plate of remainders, a prodigy of
raisins, bones and crusts, tomato skins and tea bags,
a red blotched napkin on the top, her day and week
rising in a chorus.

Aunt R saved me from hum-drum, from dwindling
to a crumb. She loved my flaws and joked them to
perfections. "Feet like canal boats—better, snails?"
"So? A high forehead shows brains."
She mocked my disasters, even made me smile.
"Calamity Jane!   Lucky you're alive."
And best, she'd point to me, insisting to my mother,
"She's got more in her one pinky than
that brother wipes away from his behind."
Mother's friends found Aunt R "vulgar, unrefined."
"She's got a mouth on her," they'd turn the other way.
To me the mouth was generous like the nose.   Both of
the same kind.

Her "nose job" made Aunt R into a Jane Wyman, more
goyischa and more "available," though
one nostril withered like a raisin, the other drooped,
a radish.   Aunt R changed jobs, had her tubes
"untangled" ("God spared her womb"), lied about
her age and married.   Stopped singing, even
"Rose O' Day." The black she dressed in was a different
black, and she grew fat, managed to have a baby and
grew fatter. Became settled—no talk of buyers cursing out
the manager—and gave up fish bones... Never cared
about her house, only that the floors were gleaming—
the pots she scoured so hard, you saw your face
hop-scotching on the metal. No furniture to speak of, only
garbage cans and boxes where she'd store mops and
brillo pads and clorox.

The son grew up, married "a real dumb-bell."
Her husband spends
days typing—what it is, no one can figure. Aunt R eats
pizza and visits doctors ("They should all drop dead")—
two or more
a week. She claims everything burns her insides—the TV screen,
the door-knob, the tree nearest the porch stairs.
She is all the time on fire and most
inside her mouth.

Commuters

In slinky toes, heels shaped like lollipops,
Manhattan women are perfect in their shoes.
Plum lipped and creamy-cheeked, they visit shops,
swish fabric over torso, hips, and choose
a pose—Billie Holiday sings the blues.
In sultry tones, she struts around her pain,
eyes moist and filmy—lovers pay heavy dues.
They try on love before the next A train.

To F# chords on bass, each woman clip-clops
before the mirror, nods and waits her cues.
The clarinet plays "hard-to-get," then hops
to "sweet-talk" triple eighths.   Now she'll fuse,
intoning peach-smooth, rasping words.   She views
her image—white gardenias, pearls, the strain
of arms forever clasping the one she'll lose.
They try on love before the next A train.

So cool in black silk pants and post-mod tops,
discreetly sprayed, the New York women ooze
Chanel, click heels in time. Not one flip-flops
over a single beat. Each shoulder, hip imbues
control. They're ready with their primped hairdos
to find "the man I love" and fly with Coltrane
or die. Flee kitchens, desks, the yearly cruise.
They try on love before the next A train.

Tight sequined sheathes—oh, how can they refuse
such breathless danger? Their breasts hold that refrain
of offbeat rhythms, the image of their muse.

They try on love before the next A train.

Eucharist

A Poor Student's Elegy
Richard Ellmann, 1918–87

> *"Something is hungry,*
> *it is not fed."*
> —*Dennis Trudel*

For years I remembered your poodle
       Daedalus
eating potato chips in rhythm
      to the voice
         O
tell me all about
Anna Livia! *I want*
    to hear…
Your eyes leapt at every word
… the loom of his landfall…

Fitful we sat
fixed in your living room
as if taking an exam
ashamed
four imperfect scholars
on straight-backed chairs
fearing softness of the couch
we didn't deserve
listening
wishing we understood or
could
might drown,
oh to be like Molly Bloom
breathing "Yes."
… and sun shines for you
Today, yes…
Or might we, like Finnegan,
wake up
and find the Escher forms
palsey-walsey
Oh I remember eating Mars Bars,
guilty,   growing fat.
Struggling with monsters

I was Ulysses.
Sorcerers whispered "Transformation,
Metempsychosis is a cinch."
Like Calypso, I cajoled *Ulysses*—
how many years?
More than seven.
Caught up in waves of erudition,
towed under by self-recrimination,
sirens singing "Refrain."
"How was St. Ambrose lured by
water?" I implored the Jesuit priest.
"Don't you know all saints love water—
where would they practice walking on?"
Keepers of secrets—Joyce, Ambrose, the Church.
No saint, I grappled with *Finnegan*,
"pebbles and rubbish… bits of glass…"
Schwitzer was *mattress*, *Albert*
maybe a *licorice* and….
"Nothing in Joyce is not deliberate,
nothing is wasted," you said,
as if I needed to know *twig*
in Anglo-Irish was "understand."

       if he could bad twig her…
I let "Proteus" lapse into ripple
not to drown
not to drown
not to disappoint you—
"good twig" all you ever…
Blasphemer, heretic I became.
       James—shames—fames
       Joyce—woise—noise
I wrote black graffiti on my carrel.
appearing one by one from
Esperanto
calling us good-naturedly to swig.
"Oh, epiphany, epiphanies—ballyhoo."
And what of you?
You stirring from inside your flowered chair
a single hand palming at a phrase
fingers close and hold, clasp
let go—
the child catching, releasing "Santa Claus."
Knowing fingers.

For years I remembered flinging a T-bone steak
hard to the floor,
the Scott Hall Union, five o'clock
after seminar.
Coming to Pound's Canto LII,
you had turned to me—
the impossible made casual
as ever—
"Learn Chinese this week with Professor Hsu."
Did I construct an ideogram or
was I the shattered carcass of a cow?
(Of *Finnegan*, David Garnett confessed,
"I understand it no more
than does a cow.")
How had I deluded you—
with desire in my hasty scribbling or
startled groping for "good sense"?
Or because you had a god inside
did you assume your tongue,
like hands, healed others of
a commonness, a lesser brain?
You seemed to be convinced
you could help us all be gods
through your tongue and theirs—
Eliot, Sitwell, Pound and
Joyce, Joyce, Joyce.

What still sticks on my tongue—
for an unfinished thesis
you awarded me
the scarlet letter A.
Oh tenderly you slipped it
carefully on my tongue
"Nothing is not deliberate,"
You dared me to swallow,
dare me to swallow even now
you are gone.
I reach out, reach across
past memory and moment.
"*Una stretta di mano*"—
Joyce ends his letters.

"*Una stretta di mano*."

263 Prinsengracht
Spaces of Memory and Despair

> O Holy Ghost, whose temple I
> Am, but of muddle walls, and condensed dust
> —John Donne, from The Litanie

Anne, 1943

Dance, to lift my arms and whirl, to jump—*jump*,
the word tugs at my breath. I welcome the surprise of sun
chirping through netted window glass. Yes, I need
a song, a beat.   Drop my opal brooch into one
palm and then the other.   Dance with every thud.

Memory of a Visitor

I life the curtain. No moon tonight   just this glare
sceping through the dark.   Opposite my window
a foreign world—burning tambourines and tapping feet.
Whiplash laughter   small bird cries a shout.   Behind
that shade something wounds. I move my pillow.

Anne, 1943

I sit still. Translate *La Belle Nivernaise*—
"je perds la chose" ... sounds tease and piroutte,   gentle
wounds I dare to think I have.   No broken bones,
only boredom.   Fear?—if I remember.   Outdoors a carriage
over-turned, an old woman gathering up the toys.

Memory of a Visitor

The detailed chart adhesived to the chartreuse wall,
the bedroom war she fought each day for grades.
Lists of imports, exports, major cities   some refuge
from the street where girls played "captive princess"
and boys played dice with knives.

Anne, 1943

We move inside each other's smell.   Mouths twitch
to smother indignities, to stifle coughs.   Eyes wander
probing a space free of elbows, the spittle raised
beneath that tongue.   The world is skin. How urine falls
inside a bucket defines the other.   Our identity.

Memory of a Visitor.
>"Find the self," the child insists, "deep inside the couch,
>down within the desk"—inside curlicues of letters,
>birthday cards. Like a prize in popcorn, I'll draw out "me."
>Move fingers over piano keys and listen for my name.
>A creaking down the hallway.   Hide inside the closet!

Anne, 1943
>God, remember I am here behind the revolving
>wall. I am the fourth.   Four women bleeding and no
>rags.   If we could thread potato skins... If—if—
>Buttons tug at button holes, a gap across my chest.
>What a nuisance, the body!   I twist my hair in curlers.

Memory of a Visitor
>One corner of the church, steps rising on a curve,
>a shelter from the wind.   Four men, faces chapped and
>haggard, crouch against the false side door try sleeping,
>their beds, stuffed garbage bags, soiled towels.   Legs tangle,
>bunch, life's merry—he plays on his penny whistle.

Anne, 1943
>I dream of trees raining in my hair.   Snow,
>crystals unraveling on my tongue and running   running,
>holding Liese's hand leaping over canals   and...
>and... love... love... love... I dream I do not
>have to dream.

Here
>Anne, forgive me for annexing your rooms,
>for living in your house I've made my own.
>If I "play house," the game is real   and you
>belong   the ghost in me
>and holy.

Clouds forming ice crystals can give rise to haloes

The angle of unknowing where mirrors intercept
in corners
        and reflections criss-cross   optics, magic
          when the face,   eyes forward,
              moves into a backward version   of itself
                and past and present fuse,
      coming and going that inseparable movement
      which upsets the world   did that winter

when my brother walked away despising
who I was   "fat sister" with tacky
diction, no memory of the critical detail,
using the entrée fork to pick up lettuce
and pulling up drooped stockings
down at ankles,   bunched in assorted
pouches   like her brain   "messy,"
I didn't resist the image   would not feel
                     anything
regarding him as—yes, infallible

and after we made the curt goodbye
and each walked down the mirrored hall
      toward opposing ends   I felt the glass stare
              forcing me to a truth.
              Inside one panel I saw him weeping,
              entirely flushed with grief,
              body huddled in that flawless coat
              and twitching side to side
              between separate points   of a disaster.

"That reflection inside me," I thought   and turned
just at the moment of his running   his running, yes, to me—
      dignity unloosened in his flapping tie
      and tremulous embrace
          and small "I'm sorry"—
that one vision tricked in the mirror   the one reality of him
                      cruelty refracting

        a faltering of love   or something close

his love, a dissolving snow, soon frozen back to crystal
which like a mirror is vulnerable to light yet

> who can find the sun
> to make his memory flow,
>   a memory convulsed by rays crueler
>   than his words—

> his brain scrupulous, a perfect crystal set,
> the words he uses faded   too deliberate.

4. Perspectives of Gender: Sister & Brother

Mozart's Sister

Nannerl's London Diary:
May 13, 1765, After a Court Concert

Lavender tints my skin like a sombre chord, like mist
in London twilight.   The Queen was kind to send the gown.
Mama would like the satin ribbons, and I would like
Theresa's strudel, to wander through the Lochelplatz.
More sweet to hear the whortle of my dear canary
than hear the Queen's quavery Handel.   Wolferl played
hard at camouflage; the organ swished like a fountain,
chords he improvised.   For the Telemann song I've tried
my own variation—awakens frowning whole notes.
Wolferl and I played it tonight.   What silly tricks
grown-ups demand.   Find notes on a keyboard covered
by a cloth! I conjure insects.   Make Wolferl guffaw.
High violin notes he has me name—allegretto.
Easy for him, never a mistake.   Yet at nine, hard
to be perfect. Always.   Thirteen years I've tried to be.
Not a prodigy, thank God.   Sneeze—it may be a G flat,
what do I know?   Know sound taps my soul like a snow-flake,
see-saws my fingers into air—I once dropped a cup....
Oh, to taste Theresa's chocolate. To be at home,
play only for deep mountain silence, chirruping birds.
Not for coarse slapping palms, the measure of Father's praise.

Leaving the hall, heard people humming—the serenade.
"Father, not mine." Wolferl grinned.   "It's hers, Nannerl's."

Each Other's Keeper

A meditation based on fragments from the letters and journals of Mary Lamb as recovered by William Hazlitt Jr., son of Sarah Stoddart Hazlitt, to whom Mary Lamb had entrusted her possessions.

Did my grandmother—did she know
back then when I was nine,
see the stitches of
predestined crime
needling through my fidgety strands
of hair, criss-crossing the swollen ridges
of my brow
branding me with matricide?

Summers, there at Blackesware,
Mrs. Field, my grandmother—and
my mother's mother, after all—
would scare me with myself.
"Polly, what are those poor crazy
moyth'red brains of yours thinking
always?"
And I so withered by her reproof, pretended
busyness, fiddled with my embroidery frame.

Plumer's manor Grandmother only "kept,"—
Charles and I "summer children,"
noblesse oblige—a shame if we displaced
a candle-stick a quarter inch or placed a finger,
however softly, on a china bowl. "Quick,"
Mrs. Field would say, "the deed is done."
I never touched that painting!   Would look
and look. Still I had no need to feel
the lady's cheek, her shimmering blue gown.
Enough to listen to her voice,
her many consolations and her praise.

She and I, we had our secret alphabet—
was that a sin?
And should I lie and say,
"This lady is not the mother I would have?"
All sins and lies my grandmother unraveled...

and poor Charles, eleven years before your birth,
the sins and lies were waiting and
the madness.

Charles—precocious always—
by four he'd learned his letters,
fingers tracing perfectly the epitaphs
on tombstones.
At twenty-one he fingered letters of blood,
the ones his sister left.
I was his teacher for both accomplishments.

"Sometimes I wish her dead,"
he wrote to Coleridge
(I in the room as always)—
three asylum visits that past year
when he was twenty-three.
Already his sister's keeper,
her "guarantee."
"A kept woman," I quipped under breath.
My shimmering blue lady laughed,
and wept from the reaches of my heart.

Charles could have had his ladies—
Fanny Kelly adored his *Essays of Elia*,
would embrace the gawky frame,
his limp no matter.
"Your wit is robust and your maladies
are charming."
Entranced by his stammer,
she considered it a "gift"
and used it for her Ophelia
at Drury Lane.

The malady "through the sister," Fanny found
too tragical,
refusing the "high honor" of
my brother's "preference,"
claiming a "prior agreement
of the heart."

Charles and I marred and married
both. (Charles enjoys such puns.)

We've had our children, too—
"dream children," maybe, or "envisioned."
Readers of our books, *Tales from Shakespeare*,
Poetry for Children, and "my special daughters,"
joining the other "girls" in
Mrs. Leicester's School.
All these children more mine than
his.   His special child was real.

Emma Isola, our adopted child,
pulsated in his blood...
Oh, Charles, poor bachelor,
she was your new beginning, the fragile
bloom on your half-century cheek,
the quick breath
that tipped your balance,
toppled your bent sky.

"Upstanding, generous—
you very gracious Lambs. Such charity—
to raise the motherless child."
Here our visitor clacking over Emma,
cradling that sentiment warm
inside his palm   waiting for nods,
a gratitude for praise   until
he caught my eye,   the eye of
"the mad sister."
Oh, fumbled at his cup,
fingers coiled into a seal.
Left palm thrusting, pushing back
"a thing"   setting a space between
our chairs.

Fence of chairs   three chairs
faces rising into flame
blood, streams of blood, trailing
through the needle's eye.
Devils on pins   pins
flickering inside my brain.
Mouths of scissors jabbing— Stop!
"Get it, do it. Now. Now."
Hissing tea pots   racking spokes,
the wheel chairs turning round, again,

quicker, more quick. I am caged   split,
cannot see, find breath.   Voices stab.
The mean to thread my eyes.
Flesh   Flesh
whorls.   Engorging fish skins... I drown.
Will not.   Cut.   Slash through hooking scales or
die into this life—
The knife, yes.   Daggers to all knaves.

I am polite about this memory,
lay out the crocheted doily
over my theatrics,
over the sizzling blood.
Later, calm apologetic,
I will say to Charles,
"It's time for my asylum."

To our visitor I say,
ignoring fist and fevered eyes,
"We have some new-made jam—raspberry—
do try some on your scone."

Unmailed Letters
Fanny Hensel to Her Brother, Felix Mendelssohn

> "... the only calling of a young woman is the state of a house-
> wife. Woman have a difficult task; the constant occupation with
> apparent trifles..."
> —Abraham Mendelssohn to his daughter, Fanny,
> age twenty-three years

1830 —Six weeks after Fanny's child is born.

Sebastian plays his mother's breast
sounding like an oboe straining
to be blown.
I sit the patient kettle drum
and thump my infant's back.

Herr Doctor orders the keyboard closed,
notation paper out of sight.
One G#, he warns, my pen transformed—
the merciless baton   and finale
to the flow of mother's milk.

Beside the piano, *voilà*! Your picture
beaming.   Rogue, you celebrate
my domestic fugue.
I will not kiss your face today,
strew blossoms on the frame
celebrating the *Hebrides* in London.

See, Felix, how I scowl—
your own "fish otter," *Fenchel*,
you called me as a child.
Like Father you approve chromatics
crocheted into a booty. *Gelinde*,
so sweet   for you.

The Patriarch enjoys my *lieder* voice
lifting out each word to save
his blurring eyes.   "Today's news—
Liszt plays triumphantly in Paris."

Très amusant, I add, "Felix argues:
Liszt has too many fingers,
too few brains."

My fingers play *allegro con moto*
with a pen.   Mother depends on her
amanuensis. And Wilhelm dotes
on his masseuse, his gifted wife
vibrating Bach "Inventions" along
each vertebra until he leaps up cured
and to his canvas once again.

My arms numb... Sebastian sleeps.
Dust motes on the mantle snared
in tunneled light.
No breeze.   In the arbor grapes hang
on yawning vines.
Only *Fenchel,* your little fish, awake
swimming toward some distant sound.

1837 —Felix discourages Fanny from composing and disapproves of her publishing.

No echo, not a sound—
all summer long I shout into the forest
carrying a beggar's bowl,
whispering "alms, one tender word."
I sing and sing "*Nacht ruht auf
den fremden Wegen*"
disappearing behind the elms.

Only the male peacock fans bright plumes.
The dowdy female hides away.
Yet... has she not a song?
Clara Schumann wrote a Polonaise at twelve
she never plays.   Nor anyone.

Our old teacher Zelter said
"Fanny plays like a man"—
a compliment?
Felix, are you praised for songs
in Opus 8 and 9—
mine?

"He composes like a woman!"
Oh, high praise!

"Music will perhaps become his profession, while
for you it can and must only be an ornament, never
the root of your being and doing... and your very joy
at the praise he earns proves that you might, in
his place, have merited equal approval."
   —Abraham Mendelssohn to his daughter
    Fanny, age fifteen years

1846 —Fanny publishes her first compositions

"The Cantor," you called me—
how many years ago?
In my old age I publish Opus One...
(Cecile, I must be yours and Felix's
sixth child... the forgotten Jew
waiting for Elijah still.
Not that I ever hear
that voice Jehovah's, Christ's.)

In Michelangelo God touches
only Adam's hand, not Eve's.
Eve not more than Rubens's goddess,
all abject curves, a sloven,
her fingers pressed beneath His wrist
apologizing for her birth.

Felix, where is your Oratorio
to Rebecca, Mary?

I need your touch, Felix,
the nectar from your soul.
Like Puck, transform my donkey's head
to human. A little extra spray
for talent.

I am your other part, as you are mine.
Always I have been your dunce,
cap heavy over ears
hands behind my head
waiting to hear "Begin."

60

What do I care for others' praise
even now... and memory is a dwindled wick
fired by a single wish.
So Goethe liked my *lied*
thinking it was yours.
"So prodigious for sixteen!"

Do the publishers want Opus One
only for your name? "Oh, Fanny H
is Mendelssohn's sister, you know."
"Hensel" as despised as Melusine?
Melusine—"too many fortes
after the crescendo,"
I reproved. You listened.
I your faithful *schuhu*, finicky
as ever, proud as any housewife
showing off her spotless rooms.

What will I have to show?
Paganini rips out the heart of his violin,
throws orange peels on stage.
I will starve my heart, refuse.
Calculate the square root of vibration
eating chocolate cake at Josty's
afternoons. Watching out the window—
There against the *schmelzglas*
colors mingle in the mottled light
and tunes.

When Henry James and His Sister, Alice, Watch Me Snipping Beans

1 — Henry

"The power to guess the unseen from the seen, to trace the implications of things, to judge the whole piece by the pattern...may... be said to constitute experience."
—Henry James

It is an action of the mind to see
the way the fingers break off stems from either
end of bean, to mark how sparing the eye
to save the edible green envelope
of seeds.   She snips the particles that cling
to stems with urgent teeth before she flings
the fragments toward the drain as if refusing
the demarcations of waste from valued part,
as if inventing her place. These atoms are hers,
raw and crisp, while others wait for cooked—
for ordinary food.   She peers at scars,
at streaks, at freckled skin along the strand
of every bean; with a knife evicts the blemish.
The knife will slide too close to flesh sometimes.
Does she remove others' flaws, counting her own?
Intent she is—flexed neck, the thrust of shoulder,
as if beans were more, as if preparing
were performance—resistance, too, the fingers twisting
vines, the fingers treading above green space.

2 — Alice

"[Experience is] only of interest and value in proportion as we find ourselves therein."
—Henry James

A martyr to the nonsense of the kitchen.
Idiotic tasks
producing tendonitis and leprosy of the soul.
She pulls the beans to pieces, stabs their bodies
for amusement.

One day her suicide from chlorophyll discourse.
Does she imagine her string bean is a minaret?
It is her tumor; her tainted womb empty
of life, of sound; her bright and palpable
affliction.
Does she journey this lowly vegetable
imagining she rides
the silent injuries of straitened womanhood?

Cringing in ignorance, she is whipped by every bean
that mocks those hands—
once quick to pantomime hauteur, now reduced
to snapping vines.
Maenad maimed by peeling off her skin and brains,
thinking her fingers sing and play on pulsing stops
beneath a reed—
that bandage hiding her own pulse and need.

Listen.
Not your armor, not your prison, not even your
green whale.
The bean does not swallow you alive, stifle
what you will—
If you choose laughter, toss it like confetti,
embrace the devious worm
and lift your face to the blue comedy
outside.

Portait of His Sister
by Guisseppe Pellezza da Volpedo (1868-1907)

Typical of how a man removes
himself from grief
employing others to feel the tragedy
he will not feel
unless he finds by dabbling at his palette
the color of lament
which reveals his talent, smoothes reality
with a fiction.

The mourner, his dead sister, is the subject—
Antonietta
suffering for the absence of herself
in a white blouse
which incises shallow bones of cheeks and brow
and intensifies the blue—
her luminescent eyes which stare beyond
the glassed-in frame.

The faded yellow pansy that she holds
whispers decay,
and the pale yellow in her cummerbund above
her spreading skirt,
a forest green, vibrant, gay, the same color
resounding in the chair
encircling her, this woman named "A Memory of
Grief," she grieving

for her brother who revels in the scrolled design
of curving hair
in the texture of the leather chair, in achieving
such a radiant shade—
this forest green which glorifies all Nature,
exalts his own, and
resurrects the deceased for others' pleasure,
for his own fame and

restores the lovely sister to her brother
to compose his grief.

The Seamstress of Flowers
After Grimms' "The Six Swans"

> *The sister encountering her brothers in swan skins, discovered*
> *the nature of their plight. Afterwards, she wept and asked,*
> *"Can't you be set free?" "We don't think so," they said. "The con-*
> *ditions are too hard. You'd have to go six years without speak-*
> *ing to anyone or laughing, and during this time you'd have to*
> *sew six little shirts for us made of asters. If just one single word*
> *were to fall from your lips, then all your work would be for*
> *naught."*
>
> —*from Jack Zipes's translation in*
> **The Complete Fairy Tales of the**
> **Brothers Grimm, I, 199.**

Starwort hangs on the sleeves of trees. Waiting.
Frost burns my skin. Thorns grate. Tonight swans fly
low. I feel my breasts shrivel, my womb, the life
I carry... must stifle self.   Fear is betrayal.
Should I fail, disloyal I am to brothers. Vile
as that step-mother   her tinseled guile our doom.

Doom of women. My husband's mother connives
my death, contrives infamy. "Accursed," she cries,
"from a despised race." At night steals into our bed,
lies close to her son, whispering her dread and love
for him.   With love, I smoothe blossoms—the moon bright
for sewing.   My swans alight. Watch from a rock.

Oh, to rock my babies—I remember one,
soft thatched head... a son, I think.   Slow, take care—
the needle slips. I dare not rip petals. Shirts
demanded whole, and whatever hurt sudden, deep,
with smothered lips I work. Keep stitching, stitching—
or brothers, in thrall to the witch, suffer my breach of silence.

Silence. The punishment of women.   Not even a stone
is silent. Not bone. Bend close and a pulse thrums.
God hums through everything we know.   Only I am mute,
a lute unstrung—without song.   What sound
describes a being bound in emptiness and pain?
Nor can fingers frame language   only flowers.

Fingers shuttling hour after hour
secretly, in dreams.   I must press hands to lap
those days the King, my husband, comes.   He taps my chest
my lips and back.   Blows "Ah" from his chest and smiles.
"Now, you!" he nods.   I mouthe—my trial—nothing.
Keep my vow.   *Another wing, another sleeve.*

I stanch desire.   Before he leaves, my husband turns.
"You need not earn my love," he says. "Your eyes speak
what you are."   I am weak from sorrow and fear.
I feel milk rising and tears.   Life trembles
inside, so God wills, and Brother swans long for rebirth.
What is life a worth—my brothers', my child's,

or mine, a mother denied?   Dumb when she smeared
my mouth with blood.   "Monster" I appear.   Why
couldn't I cry, "Innocent. She steals my child"? Where
my babies—where? Life twists and knots like thread.
I hear—dreadful—their wings beat on the ground.
Beating, pounding in my womb. Must ... I fall.

"Six shirts on the bough ready," I would call.
I must call.   I want to call.
"Yes, seven years. Trust me. Do not fly—fly
away. Wait for birth. You know I do not lie."
I cannot rise.   I can say nothing.
Wait.

1845, After the Last Volume

—from a letter written by William Wordsworth to Lady B.

As if Nature were an infernal blank
as blank as this accursed paper—
empty, snarled as Dorothy's mind.
Vacancy deep as death—
John and Thomas, Catherine.   Now
Joanna. Accidental loss or loss
governed by a physical decline—what matter?

No "sunny glimmerings" of linnet,
mosaic flight of butterfly.   Gray
suffuses lake and fell, the leaves
are still, though I can hear the wind.
The world is difficult to breathe,
a thin smoke that spreads into our
very souls.

The breath of brain is stilled, the fire of
words, the blessing—she who wore
her "woodland dress," whose voice gave
voice to me.   I called her "Lucy,"
"dearest Friend," described "the shooting
lights of her wild eyes." Now she is
wilderness herself.

Convulsive writhings alternate with song.
Sometimes she mutters verses of her own.
The wanderer sits vacant in her wheelchair
raging at the sky.
Once quick flighted fingers—latticing
pie crust, hemming shirt cuffs, tender
with the roots of gathered flowers—
are frantic, aimless. They clutch,
unclutch at nothing.

This morning, stretching out her ring finger,
she grasped my left hand with her right,
till I slipped off my wedding ring,

placed it where she wished.
Her right fingers caressed the ring
over and once again.
I am dumb with love and grief.
All words are out of place.

5. The Eye Inside the Storm

Scourge for Accidental Voyeurs

National Public Radio Broadcast—from Germany: Neo-Nazis spit on crippled cyclist—call him "half-man" and "parasite." The man later commits suicide. In a civil court action, a family is awarded "vacation costs" for "pain inflicted by hotel policy"; that is, by allowing handicapped guests use of the beach, where in consequence, said family was exposed to "ugliness, shame, and horror."

Handicapped   capped teeth
and dunce cap brain   the hand-shake
a shaking hand   absurd in frantic
reiteration   antennae fingers
point and point   to nothing

Handicapped ugly slow unclean—
vermin crawling over under skin
cooties parachuting down each hair
dirty thoughts twisting in the coiled
nematodish gut thick and yellow
as chicken soup   devouring
your blood   drowning claws choke
your very swallow

Handicapped lopped off pieces   splintered
glass twisted spokes wires loosed
from circuits   broken pipes and bars
and screws   hailstones falling on
your face   and in your path
unbalancing a posture   forcing
indirection jagged gaping
smashed unfinished cracked   any
where   clock with spastic tick rattling
piano with stuck keys jig-saw
puzzled nothings   without parts

Handicapped can hide   twisted toes
inside of leather   warts and moles
underneath sleek cloth   the sawed-off
breast of the Amazon flaunting ripe
prosthesis   the innocent glass eye

deceptive cast-iron hip
secret   until you poke around

tap tap   there it is stuttering and wheezing
the rag-taggle tongue   sli-pshod
bronchial tubes and lungs   manic
DNA and molecules amuck sub-
atomic particles conspire   the devil
how they shape-shift
invisible

Handicapped aliens   a threat
cysts zoom   jewels of pus splattering
on the wall   wrinkles gavotte
to Bach Inventions   bones   clap themselves
to dust   exquisite crescent nails unravel
then epidermis   arteries and veins   vile weeds
embedded in the musculature   oh yes
let the body dissolve
and certainly the hand   how pure—
it can neither punish nor caress
here it is   the empty glove
holding   Beethoven's ear

Coffee Break

Gaunt attenuated   tipping out of space
each time he moved
Beard a palimpsest—tarnished silver
grated with burnt iron
Wild hair   distraught antennae
wrenched by sound   the chair legs
dragged along the floor
tap tap of a coin   Apocalypse—
the ambulance outside wails and
wails again   Oh stop stop
Hairs rise   nerves corkscrew
to cascade each decibel
a hammer to the brain   He shudders

The ear phones cancel nothing.
He fiddles with the metal head piece,
jerks the wires of each ear-piece,
head steering every whichway.
Frenzy of colliding messages.
Body signaling or trying,
trying something.   Not like a bird
with broken wings that attempts
to fly.   Nor like a baby, arms outspread
legs sputtering to a tremble.
Not any motion of water, fire,
wind. Near like a rope that tries to lasso,
misses again, again.

One hand grips the table—grips and grips
and misses   Misses the chair   Misses
Si- si- sits.
One palm staggers across the cup while
the other hand lifts from the bottom
till quavering coffee splashes the mouth
Head oscillates   a semaphore
with nothing to direct
Each of his legs a separate agenda and
vying   whipping out vaudeville routines
non-stop   frantic like every other part
except the voice   scratching a whisper

so faint that the finger must tick tick
on the glass to show the muffin it craves
and   a wonder the head slows
nods and nods at the clerk

Nod to yourself   call him avatar   prophet
        Turn away, forget. Take it easy.
So easy to glide the coffee cup
straight to your mouth   sip nice
        and steady
when you want him to hear your scream,
    when you want him to feel your grip,
            you clutching him fast and faster
                    in a wild tarantella   and   circling   circling
                    till the earth finally   stops.

pin-prick

a nuisance really   nothing like a wound—
less the hurt than failure   the no-win game
when I locked into the double seat with
Elinor last name ending in a B like mine
was the victim of the alphabet in 3A1
placed as we were in seats by letter and

Elinor never absent   trouble a constant
any time   the criminal assured
optimum health   by drawing blood
iniquity so easy   my left arm
her colony   each nick a dotted flag
her designated sovereignty nor could I find
escape or else I feared rejected safety and

the game seemed separate from the player

pain always a surprise from that especial
source   Elinor scarce a felon
no threatening eyes   smug triumph
round the mouth following the event
her thrusts quick and neat without
glee or anger   the jabs grew commonplace

part of the school routine   sometimes I felt
obliged longing for the puncture on the day
Elinor refrained   did I prefer serenity
of the wounds to Mrs. B's wild missiles as
in the middle of explaining the reason
for monsoons or the reason for anything
our teacher would grow frenzied   throw rulers

pens and chalk   blame class inattention

Mrs. B. refused all questions   ignored raised hands
from blacks   and even though Elinor knew answers
looked smart   each pleat of her skirt knife-sharp
middy blouse gleaming   whiter for the polished
mahogany of face   her six braids tight in bird barrettes
torso high and straight as a ballerina *en pointe*

her eyes too stretching   beyond blackboard
through wall to world   never looking sidelong
at me   before or after the pin   or in between
yes   once she looked   even smiled
that time after I'd been summoned to the board
I prize pupil   white with high forehead and glasses
had to solve the fraction 7/8 x 11/3

as impossible for me as returning volleyballs

until Mrs. B. turned slantwise reaching for a lozenge
and Elinor mouthed the answer to me   smiling   I mad-
dashed the numbers   perfect Mrs. B. announced
the one pupil who pays attention   after which
Elinor stopped impaling   who knows why
maybe because I made her paper dolls for free

didn't charge the 2 cents others had to pay and
crayoned their faces bodies   brown   made
their dresses wonderful   splashy
with flowers of bright orange   purple swirls

Threat

The face was in her head and everywhere,
      walked up and down the steps, turned sideways
      on its nose, eyes blurring into shadow, mouth crushed—
      or rising as a genie, all face, it loomed over rooftops
      growing in her brain. Sometimes
      the whole city contracted into one short city block,
      bodies in silhouette at either end   stretched taut
      ready to break. Crack! Asphalt and concrete splinter.
      The whole city dissolves.

Face—demon, trickster, Jack-in-the-Coffin Box   hiding,
      popping out—a sign in the coffee shop.
      Look through the letter "D" in doughnut. There's the nose.
      Dancing on the Venetian blind, yes, mouth and ears.
      In an alleyway, the head rolls down cobblestones,
      jumps up on a window ledge   and leers.
      She thought herself to be anthropologist of heads,
      practicing a smart indifference
      not to grow insane.

Sleeping became strategy—how to mystify the face.
      Consecrated foods, honey grahams and nectar,
      formulas to outface the dark. "Will power,"
      declaimed a voice. A pillow by her bed
      a barrier to it, the pattern on her sheet
      an interruption to his efforts. She needed to face him,
      deface him. He must not wander in her dreams.
      In daylight she was safe   from his grimacing
      through mirrors. Nor would he / it (puff-puff) rise
      from underneath the rug. He tended to avoid her house
                    unless . . . .

Awakening from a dreamless sleep, she felt the eyes
      inside her head, irises and corneas both cold potato white,
      eyes potato buds everywhere.
      She feared an excess of success, a triumph too persistent
      in rearranging features—call them faces.
      Lately, all faces that she met were somewhere
      else, cavorting in a psychic space that altered and
                  recontoured,

a flimflam of mutation
where eyebrows dipped inside a sea of skin
dissolving like dried milkweed.

Eyes, nose, mouth muddled in her brain,
       lips pouting on a cheek, nostril taunting
       from a forehead split in half.
       Sometimes, remembering the Aztecs,
       she conjured up masks which walked up and down
       the supermarket aisle. Nor could she describe his / the face.
       She knew and didn't . . . and, of course, they were annoyed.
       If she had visions of a face,
       it was all her own fault.

"Certainly" (they said) "you should have some self-control."
       She had told them he / it was white, black with rage;
       black, white with rage   and burning, trying to be cool.
       The body? Yes, he / he had one. Figured like an urn
       silvery and sleek, secreting fire.
       Oh, yes, she had described the body arced for lunging,
       bulleted fists and head a cannon ball.
       "Some fear is genuine," they said, "if restrained.
       Untainted by the imaginative mind."

The face was in her head and everywhere.
       They never saw it, didn't dare, were
       annoyed—and, of course, no one looks at faces anymore
       or should   till the face appeared in schools on blackboards,
       the face smiled inside stars
       on flags—yes, corneas and irises, cold potato white, and
       smiling teeth like cattle cars
       chugging toward a void   nose rooting like a pig
       eager for souls. They saw the face in dreams and mirrors,
       spread out on their beds and inside
              the flowers in their yards. They asked her,
              tried to ask her what to do,
              were   voiceless. Yes, their faces lost,

              they had lost their heads.

The Quest
A Reply to T.S. Eliot

Five o'clock, fading light on cobblestones,
I look at lovers under the umbrella.
The umbrella is purple, yellow, green.
The rain is dotted sugar-fine, a dance
of drops in a painting by Seurat.

The lovers *pas de deux* uphill
gliding in silhouette, confiding
nuances. They share a single smile.
Bodies tinselly with secrets
toss sparks in small bouquets.

The rain grows flowers and the lovers fade.

Leaves drown, signs on storefronts.
Windows shrink inside brick walls.
I feel my woman's bones
whittling down the seasons.

No reason for decay if I
resolve   abide as Fisher Queen
till Parsifal heals my wasted frame.
I will rise   Hyacinth Girl
from under the umbrella.

The lovers are not faded.
Parsifal's hair is black and shining
curved to nape and brow with humor.
Mouth confident and open to a perfect space
is innocent of toothache,

does not wince at stooping bodies,
hands deciphering the shape of need
inside of ruthless garbage. Does not clench
against the listless wait for shadowy roots,
the rain that seeps and eats and muddies.

When had Parsifal stopped to taste
how arid is the peach,

played tunes with sea-shells, listened
to their call, longed for a whiff of breeze
along the fire escape?

Has he ever felt the veils of dark
ensnaring corridors and eyes?
When was he ever tempted to slip off
earphones listen
turn off screens   and pray?

His skin is icing on a cake
layered opulent and glossy.
I saw his lacquered fingernails.
I am embarrassed for his ease
and   I admit   disturbed.

What knowledge of the sangreal
is possible to him?   Sense of healing
or deliverance?
He has whitened teeth and drives a Porsche.

I will not be the girl under the umbrella.

City lights shiver in dark puddles,
start to pulsate in the downpour.
I huddle, briefcase to my chest, and fish.
Where are the tokens in my pocket?
Aging Fisher Queen fishing—

Under tissues, coins, strange fragments
shore beneath my fingers.
Without elation or surprise, I trace the contours
of the grail. Feel young.
"Poor trick," I smile into the rain.

                    "When will history begin?"

So much is upside down

like Bat—hooked claws, he's made his bed,
patagium cozy warm. On spreading limbs
Sloth forms her hammock. Face raised to the sky,
she sleeps or munches berries sluggishly has sex.

Mandeville—that liar—reports a far-off land
where men are headless, ears hanging down to toes.
Children say "Dig a hole through the earth.
There in China, feet discuss the weather in mid-air."

In Senegal babies are naturally born old.
Foreheads wrinkle with worries of a century.
Limbs thin like straw unraveling from baskets.
Only their mouths are big and wide   gape
like empty bowls.

My feet are walking ahead of my head. Before
I can reach, acknowledge it's mine,
my head disappears into shadowy rills. And look,
a gull poised on a puddle standing on its head.

Like coupled birds, a man and a woman plummet—
heads askew, limbs flounder in the air. Gasp—
splinters of yellow eyes flash from the sky,
tidal flames of asphalt, wood, and glass.
Charred hairs nestling on an arm turn ash.

Dead fish go belly-up, while cats
belly-up and wait   that lovely stroke.
Umbrellas tipping over in high wind,
ribs sprout from canopies   as spokes,
turning on a spattered wheel.

Why Michelangelo would have us lift and turn,
strain the first and second vertebrae in necks
to view the muscled angels on the Sistine Chapel...
Is heaven only for those who lose their heads?

Old and scrawny, huffing—thin mackinaw
and hands ungloved, a little man heaves snow and

snow from stairs ascending to the health club
where members stride on frantic treadmills before
a dash to offices with ergonomic chairs.

Yesterday we rescued three new-fallen birds,
claws rigid, beaks hopelessly curved inward,
raw-skinned.   Bare tracings of wings,
small breath.   Today three try, one rises.

"Heads or tails?" he said and I said "Both."
I said, "Children delight in standing on their
heads   to set the world   P.
                                        e   U
right   i
                                d

       s

6. Illuminations from Other Spaces

Planetary Pantoum
Glyphs on Mars

Across Phobos, fearful rock-fish moon,
grooves tilt, repeat in narrow bands.
Embryo moon, hunched Deimos, quivers—
glint in the bog-dusk, salmon sky.

Grooves tilt, repeat in narrow bands—
like petaled comets, whorls lift from the crater.
Glint in the bog-dusk salmon sky,
aureole fluting plays on polar ice-caps.

Like petaled comets, whorls lift from the crater.
Spiraling canyons above, colossal pyramids;
aureole fluting plays on polar ice-caps,
Sudden... mist, clouds massed like granite, wind.

Spiraling canyons above, colossal pyramids,
rocks gouged with twined canals, script of dendrites.
Sudden... mist, clouds massed like granite, wind.
Lightning streaks cross regoliths, embrace.

Rocks gouged with twined canals, script of dendrites—
embryo moon, hunched Deimos, quivers.
Lightning streaks cross regoliths, embrace
across Phobos, fearful rock-fish moon.

Café Appassionato

—for Jack

As if bark once shed, the bough
hollowed out itself, spread and
deepened into domed recess
honing a sacred niche, like a song
just under breath, a mantra stirring
wings beneath shared fingertips.

Fingers enlace a cup, fold waffled
paninis. Others trace pencils into thought,
page gathering words from light
on an empty plate, leaf-glow,
leaves fingering window glass. Fingers
converse, lift spoons of foamed latté.

Froth seeping out of cups, warm
cheese ruffling edges of lavash—
espresso-maker whooshing, timid
laughter, the boy polishing
tea canisters and the sandwich-girl
with purpled hair enjoy

mispronouncing French. Signs
set on the poster board—*Our Town*
plays in the neighborhood,
T'ai Chi—at my house, Fridays,
how to join Sunday's peace march…
The reader pauses, "take-out" in hand.

Motion and stillness—fingers
tease out riddles inside the skin.
Everything is growing. Swirly flowers
bulge from thick ceramic cups,
tinseled buds on wired stems bloom
atop a mobile. The sleeping baby grows

and the couple sharing pasta.
In jars heaped biscotti rise in dunes,
raspberry brambles, scones.

Staged clementines—á la Cézanne—
grow rounder in their sea-green tray.
The wooden paneling grows florid,

the tree opening to who we are,
the passion

Visiting Philadelphia USA
Among the Homeless

From Independence Hall at Chestnut
to Christ Church and the Printing House,
the Franklin Institute of Science, catch
old Ben, his capacious head ascending,
mouth lifted like a benevolent Cheshire cat
teething maxims: "Early to bed..." and so on.

The Free Library is also Ben's—
sleeping there till nine p.m. is possible
three days a week unless you mind
fluorescent lights, occasional sounds of
pages flicked and rattled, the press of
Windsor chairs. That carpet thick as a mattress.

More restful, the Quaker Meeting House.
"Inner light" less an eyestrain and nothing to
half-read. The head naturally droops
in prayer, and gray walls drab the willful
presence, guards reluctant to evict you from
your God till five o' clock.

Ghosts at Fairmount mansions
are well-preserved and never miss their tea,
the teapot shaped like a house with dolphin spout.
At dinner time in periwigs and silken hose,
they eat roast beef on Wedgwood plates.
Entranceways are balanced with false doors.

A symmetry at Strawbridge and Clothiers
just as summer light dapples cobblestones.
Left hip thrust, two jutting points for breasts,
La Belle Dame mannequin in sequined dress
entices from her window.
Outside on the curb a woman sprawling in pink rags.

Light skulks in city of dark alleys,
shadows twisting underneath iron railings
and at Locust and Eighteenth against a corner wall,

a spidery man is spinning down the stars;
sweet melody unfurls from his recorder
like nebulae. Not a dollar bill in his turned-up cap.

Borders bookstore, ten p.m. just closing
when I leave with a paperback in bag.
There on Walnut beside the door dragging along
his quilt, one wise guy rising from the huddle,
laughs, "She cover her se'f in words so
fine, she don't need no umbrella—c'ept it rain."

In my room at the Latham, six floors from
the street, someone has turned up the lamp,
turned down the sheet—a wide luminous V.
A chocolate in red foil is gleaming
from my pillow. Floral drapes embroider darkness.
On my bedtime page, words jeer in the light.

In Philadelphia liberty bells are turned
into pretzels, and summer's melon boats,
displayed on carts, raise toothpick patriotic flags.
The homeless are polite, wait for silvers.
Do I squat with them or tear down
the chandeliers?

Tabernacles in the City

Market

Aphrodite rising on these waves of apples
Gaylas from New Zealand   Fuji, Braeburn.
    Bending, lifting, her body sails and dips,
    hands reaching into crates
    arms spreading like slim oars.
From wooden-slat boxes heaped and toppling over,
she singles out each apple, fits it in her palm,
arranging the separate fruit in tiers.
    Choruses of red and green, pale yellow
    sing white blossoms, trees and sun.

The young girl smiles at every fruit, at her design
and is like an apple, hair red, close-cropped.
    Her mouth savors the taste of each new voice,
    eyes beaming when someone is close by.
    "Yes, Grannie Smith—good with a mild cheddar."
Her short hair petaled like a flower ebbs and flows
with the framing of her words, head tilted to her listener,
attuned to every sound—to the wonder of it all.
    "Ah," she says about her hair when we comment
    on the style. "It was I myself who cut it."

"The rest is with a friend   in treatment. It makes a fine wig
and so loud that God himself must listen."

Underground

Outbound trains twist on criss-crossed tracks,
    writhing in dark tunnels whining, screeching.
Doors open with a gasp, engines heave.
The platform, inescapable and forever, waits—
noise and sweat and grime inside of doughnuts,
newsprint, designer suits and hair; inside the photos
on tunneled walls promising great e-dates, MBA degrees.

Wait, another sound. Listen. A recorder
    playing Handel, each note orderly and clean
    liking itself and what comes next,
        riding over entrances and exits, the chuffing wheels,
Music implacable.   Serene.
    Hunched over his stand, the player curves into a bass clef,
    his goat feet hidden behind the plate for coins.

Commuters relax portfolios and bags, forget
the kernels of popcorn moving toward their mouths,
lose hollows under eyelids, fluorescent pallor.

    They stop waiting.   It's already here—Orpheus-Pan
    come to pull them out—Hades,   the whole crew.

The Irish Jewish Museum, Dublin, 1999

Numbers 3-4 Walworth Road, near…
Yes, miss it   you could entirely
dissolving through the scrim of rain,
the commonplace of brick row houses,
door low to pavement, the half-step
entrance taunting your reluctance to be
meshpocheh with this Celtic Diaspora
so far removed from Vilnius or Scala,
Delancey Street or Sunnyside in Queens
where your grandfather secretly kept goats.

You turn the knob.   Dark sky funnels through
the dim passage   and raindrops. A single lamp
beside a guest book.   "Wh'ar ye be from?"
Níl aon tinteán mar do thinteán
féin. (There is no fireside like your own—
I learn this later.)   At one corner of the desk
baggy trousers, legs sprawled wide, a man half-
squints, floppy sweater open to your tale,
plaid cap tilted for mild interrogation.
Why do I remember—see—the steady creases

my father pressed into his pants each night?
Leopold Bloom—what did Joyce know? Think of
Molly cooking the Sabbath meal. Too funny.
Estelle, the Irish maid I loved, feared
kashrut, matzoh brie, gefillte fish.
Picked at lettuce leaves spread out on cellophane.
At Saint Mary's (Estelle took me there for mass),
the nuns blessed my doll, Patricia. And who would not
be Irish?   Judy Garland at rainbow's end,
G.B. Shaw promising *Back to Methuselah*   and Yeats.

Jews and Irish—*Abie's Rose*.   The Tuatha De Danann,
respected fairies, were students of Dedan,
Abraham's grandson, gifted in Torah and magic.
The museum is hardly respectable. Not clean.
The satin chuppah riddled with black specks
is torn.   Such a scrabble of objects, rag-tag display.
Goblets, one shofar, a tarnished wrist-watch—

belonged to an Asher Lowe, Cork dentist.
A dwarf microscope—why? The sign too faded.
Three glass cases of tefillin. Black leather straps,
black boxes, warnings to the righteous—
how to place the straps, how to pray, the need
for darkening each strip to sanctify the forehead
and left arm.   In a top hat, Professor Cohen the prophet.
The poster declares on March 5, Rathmines,
he will foretell your future by pressing fingers
to your skull.   Carrie Seidman, "Bat Mitzvah Girl,"
in a photo with her twin, Charles, who waves his tallit
at me.   Clipping about a pogrom, 1904—Limerick.
Mishmash of lives.   Bottom drawers of who we are

open.   Booming voice, brogue thick as barley soup—
Briscoe's yarmulke is wreathed with shamrocks.
Lives in Israel now.   Here to trace the ancestors for
nine grandchildren—almost ten. Booming guffaw,
Briscoe recalls Aunt Bessie. "Knocked him clear down,
that customer. Had called her husband 'Sheeny.' No
sooner than she picked him up. Made him shake her
hand." "Jews manage," says the volunteer who helps
with the research. "Whatever *chozzerai*—look at 'genetic'
food, soy challah, maybe, or pigs DNA in berries,

the rabbis bless it all. Yes."   Hitching up his straggling
pants, Briscoe looks for his overcoat someplace near
the Menorah.   Three-thirty, *meshpocheh* exodus.
Rain battering Victoria Street.   Rain whips at my legs.
Rain drowning cobblestones on Portobello Road.
Rain soaks my brain.   Midsummer.   I shiver.
In August my father ate in sweaty underwear, so tired
he spooned his lunch out of the pot still standing.
In the kitchen the mezuzah dangles crooked,
a missing nail.   A red box of Kosher Salt always damp.

Where is the bus? The tales?   Uncle Al, a "bouncer,"
at Madison Square Garden... Cousin Fran who claimed
she'd won a prize for skating.   My third grade teacher,
Miss Boyle, told me to skip dodge ball.   "Too dangerous
with glasses."   Mrs. McGowan removed her glasses when
she smiled. Crocheted doilies bought her husband Pall Mall
cigarettes.   The umbrella is too small.

Side to side I step, back and forth. Cold.
I never danced the hora or tried Irish step
dancing.   The bus.   And we are running.

The Children of Ireland

A pool of shallow water formed like a cross
above a blue and green tiled floor,
heaven and earth inside the rippling stream.
Nave of grass bordered by white basins of
red geraniums
in this chapel, the Garden of Remembrance
at Parnell Square,
monument to patriots and saviors.

The altar holds the Children of Lir
turned and turning into swans
beautiful in pain,
one leg plunged fierce into the ground
struggling to stay human.
Arms, intertwined, flail against the sky,
one already feathering as wings.
The dreadful end of childhood an ecstatic song
breathed into chiseled marble.

Along the grassy rim two girls in jeans leap-
frog, flip-flop, roll in merry tussle, suddenly
come still, edge toward the pool.
Crouching side by side, they fling spittle after
spittle into the moving waters.

Southwards on O'Connell Bridge
chalk cartoons sprawl on pavement,
listless figures, pink and blue and green—
undoggy dogs, unpetaled flowers, faces
dead-pan even as they're born.
The boy—sturdy, eight or ten—draws as
he might add sums or spell out words,
again and yet again.

Beside him is a hat for "change."
He sketches at command anything you name—
plant or creature all the same
here on Liffey's edge.

Walled in a deep valley two dark lakes,
Glendalough, where St. Kevin prayed,

words ascending as "a living flame."
Four ancient churches span six centuries of
devotion, and in the graveyard high stone
crosses stretch, stretching out their arms to
"Come, come."
In August sun the Wicklow mountains loom
like witches' caps and broom-sticks dancing wild.

Barefoot Hannah runs up and down these hills
darting between rocks and fallen trees,
fingering her yellow hat like a propeller,
steering the straw edges of the brim
ready to travel to the sky.
Journey over, she sits on muddy ground
where inside a hollow stone, she makes rain-water
soup, stirring it with a branch of rowan
and chanting magic runes.

Hannah, three years old, who solemnly recites
Wordsworth for tourists on the Bus Eirann
and makes daffodils appear.

From his highchair at the Lydon Restaurant,
the baby chants
by escalating fore and middle fingers
across his lips. He will not smile at grown-ups
who say "Give us a smile,"
nor pretend amusement at their "peek-a-boos,"
entirely concentrated on his bubbly hum

like the older children on King and Mercer Streets,
straight-backed and immaculate in stripes and plaid,
who ignore the passersby and refuse to eye
the jeweled and pastried windows or smug mannikins,
so intent on listening for their parts
on horn-pipe, accordion, guitar—
not even nodding at a coin.

On Gardiner Street the gangly boy too distant
for these tunes,
listens only to slow wheels of the carriage
he pushes for his mother

while she holds another baby in her arms
trailed by two small children
marching with steadfast loyalty

moving like the step-dancers at the Galway Siamsa
where boys and girls refuse the carefree turn
of arms and torso,
the extravagance of dismantled time.
Dancing feet tap druid messages
tender and defiant, heart-beats
merging with the living sap, the stones
of earth.

7. Transparencies of Self

Tachyonic Toss #1

for Frank and Fritjof Capra

"The desire of the pebble for release
is more than mine."
I should have told him then
(Didn't I know?)   he insisting that
my flinging stones in water
showed Freudian reversal
while I watched the universe
displaced   moving outward
from the boredom of his hunt.

Pebbles in the pond are Mercury
and Venus pulled toward a core
of energy so deep
they plunge to another universe
where "a stone's throw" can never
end   and this arm still contemplates
design, making future time
predictable as parabola
and not reverberation.

You stir the waves and cannot sense
how far and when you will arrive.
Diaphanous spirals drift in space,
tilting discs with shaded centers
clustered by a film of stars
contracting and dilating:
yoked darkness or the burst
of amniotic sac becoming light.

I am not the thrower of the pebble.
The pebble picked me up,
dumped me in the middle of this
                    POEM
a hologram for pebbles which I cannot
find   the "I" still floundering
behind the force that plays us both.

The radiating plash embracing
folds of spheres   Siva-Shakti merge,
mandalas rising, spread.
Let lovers ponder the curve of pebbles.
Children toss them in the water
fierce to scare up life.

Hieroglyphic of Bast

for Joscelyn

Eyes green tides illumined by moon-glow,
Eyes like the moon   awakening to night,
  telescope the sky for stars and owls,   plumb below
   for rabbit scrapings,   birds and mice,
         however slight.
Limbs sleek and silent—one   two batons—lift
  majestic on the bough.   Leaves and petals
   sotto voce, trill.
      Covert, a nightingale sifts
  pollen from a rose.   The arched body settles
   on a branch   tail spiraling a seductive maze,
   each ear attuned like an inverted V,
    till even whisper lulls.
      A musky fragrance plays
upon the dark,   and the form devolves into a tilted G.

Dawn flutters
     eyes sliver to yellow-orange beams.

Limbs taunt   ears tremulo   wary of human schemes.

A Song for Charmbell

Counting cats to dream
      I see her dance-leap through the clover
      carousel the cherry tree
      and balance-beam along the fence
      applauding every new achievement
      with a raised tail.

How can I slide to darkness when
      I find her lolly-doodling
      in the morning sun
      orange maps along her ears and neck
      each sly white trickle of fur waiting for
      my touch?

Why does she move against my heart
and sing adagio balalaika thrums?

Why does she loop me in her silence
      so I stay awake
      counting what has neither shape nor measure
      only the soft clawing on the blanket's nub?

She was put to sleep at seventeen
on Tuesday, a soft August night,
      that same month we kidnapped her,
      our changeling,
      from Hannibal, the Scot,
      fierce mother cat who clawed and bit
         to keep her own

         Faerie
    who sniffs unhappiness away from skin
        licks fingers into giving
    who twining round through ankles, feet
        coaxes to shared mischief
        surprises a wild thought.

         Faerie
        eyes seeing beyond Necessity, eyes pointed to
        No Time

all being hunched to magnify
the Cosmos
all motion through vast motion-
loss.

The Chinese Emperor preferred his wind-up
nightingale
of sapphire, diamond, ruby,
though it only sang one tune.
The natural bird his Highness declined:
"Paltry gray," he said, "and unpredictable."
She sang impromptu and whatever was in her heart.

The real nightingale sang Death back to his Garden
and saved the Emperor's life.

Charmbell
I save your life outside me
with this song-tomb.
Each night through darkness
I count your arcing flight,
I count your grace.

Chipmunk

Lonely in July when houses stare and wait—
    no voices. Leaves so cloistered intimate
    a world of sadness, wish skirmishing with need.
        Promised fruit abort, starlings peck out seeds.
        We eat our hearts out before we can create.

No teeth, and yet my heart is gone—too late
    to grow another when by some sleight
        of vision, a displaced pebble, this figure is decreed.

Brambly tail, mosaic stripes, netsuke head—each trait
    so lustrous clear, I feel I've borne him, relate
    as kin. He breathes back life as mutual deed
        and while I breathe, disappears. Had we agreed
        it was enough, our differences and fears too ornate?

When Turnips Turn Up Poems

At last they've prodded me—oh, quite polite—
way way back into the last drawer where
I consult with stray thumb tacks,
a stapler without a spring,
a muddled pad, spirals all unspiraling.

　　We live among crumbs, damp aspirins,
　　a piece of cellophane, one blazing page,
　　grades—all red—1969.

In 1970 I owned a wall—
something there is that loves a wall;
it was my gentle drum,
my Ouija board, a screen that showed
the lake of Innisfree magenta at mid-day.
A shaft where caverns rose and
disappeared as pleasure domes
along the river Alph.

I was praised
for painting Shakespeare's head on
pumpkins, for skilled cartography—
raised, contoured maps of countries
spied by Gulliver and More.
Professors were amazed—a duel I staged
to baroque dance with Beowulf
and Grendel's dam.

Bark paintings of the Aborigines
I used as backdrops for a novel
student version of *The Wasteland*.
Another class devised exotic flowers
in a heart-shaped bowl—Rappaccini's
garden. And how many told me
Moby Dick "just came alive" after
they had role-played Captain Ahab
and his psychiatrist!

　　Students marveled at my wisdom
　　expressed on themes by riddle,

paradox, a fable flourished
with a calligraphic symbol or cartoon.

They rewarded all my efforts
with index cards and rubber bands,
a chair to swivel on—around, around
until grey walls became a baby blue.

    I did not need the capsule flagon
    whished to covert lips like Hugh,
    my office mate, who taught
    "Literature of the Enlightenment."

One year they changed my office.
Alone I was—above encapsulated
cobalt (stored by Chemistry)
safe, I was assured (by Physics)
from lethal rays. I was not safe
from missives lodged in cracks
beneath the door. "Walden is a bore
and subversive." "Whitman is a fag."

    How might a student reflect like Alice in
    Through the Looking Glass, or
    contemplate with Brecht and Galileo
    the moving cosmos? Understand
    the death of Socrates?

In a vellum envelope on engraved paper,
a brief note questioned why I didn't
attend workshops in "Using the Computer
to Enhance Creative Arts."

During my sabbatical one year
the ROTC moved in and occupied my space,
removed the poster "In a Gentle Way"
(Gandhi smiles) "You Can Shake the World."
Tore down the swooping collage
my daughter made at three—acorns,
yarn and macaroni skip over
spangled fields.
Books from shelves were pitched in corners,
puddled at the door.

Nothing to read—this pad is empty.
Nothing except the list of grades.
On the open stapler I tap mantras
to the albatross, feed on honey-dew—
sun-light gleaming through wooden cracks.
Know, I am cautious and discreet.
Though thin, cellophane enough
disguise. Besides I'm prepared.
Thumb tacks and squiggly wires.
True, pencil shavings congregate but
slowly. Still I write.
            One day the word
                              jumps out.

The Readers

1. The Butcher's Daughter

Maps along the sawdust floor shift with
feet, wooden crates, carriages and pull toys.
Trails uncover matted feathers, snips of flesh,
a chip of bone glinting from dried blood.
Ribs tapestry the wall. A flank of beef, rivered
in fat, jabs a shoulder of veal.

"Remove the end piece from the rump."
The knife blade skates along the rim
lifting a translucent curve.

In a darkened corner on stool's edge,
an old man plucks and plucks the bird.
Its head, twisted, hangs loopy to one side.
Across from him where the counter ends,
sawdust thins to a cleared space, a metal chair.
The girl sits calm   out of reach.

Behind her wieners—ropes and ropes—
bob in back of her frizzy curls.
She is pallid among the frantic reds and

reading. Reads *Honey Bunch, The Bobbsey Twins,*
swallowing books without a pause,
never lifting her lowered head, scarcely
touching finger to page. Bundling letters
into words.   Nine-year old Shirley Hand
dances through *The Wizard of Oz* while

the chicken skips, the chicken stutters,
the headless chicken
resisting death.

2. The Stationer's Daughter

Though asleep when Sam came home, asleep
when he set out again, she knew the whole routine. Deep
in her soul's core, these images she would not lose.

Body tensed, he bolted chain mail on the doors each night,
locked divided parts, heavy clink, then left the store,
returning to "business"—the morning papers—in half-light

of day and day's tomorrows—to dusty notebooks, a floor
and walls reeking chloroethylene, the dazed heat
from Maury the Cleaner next door. That long day's stupor

the child felt, reading in the phone booth, that seat,
her usual place after school. Book or magazine, she turns a page
to find some exit, entrance, melody, an off-beat

tune to these 4/4 afternoons. Her impending rage
perfect as the stripes, she remembers, across the tiger's back
when he, so agile, shifted, turned, reversed, slathering in his cage.

Printed words refuse to hold her breath, all these listless as stacks
of unsold cards there lisping under the register. The child knows
she belongs to no landscape, day or year. Feels such lack

in body, ancestry or fate, she will never outgrow—
unless—oh—she grow shameless, fierce as sunlight.

Sam, her father, sweeps as he hums in polished shoes.

The Immutable

"Fontenelle compares the beliefs of the ancients in the immutability of the celestial bodies with the belief of a rose protesting that, as long as roses can remember, no gardener ever died."
　　　　　　　—Ernst Cassirer

Of course, they never die—the long parade
of habits, persistent memories, the charade
which mimics, gestures, teases us to enter
ambivalent conviction, prescribes the center
for our being—reminders like the address book,
an antique candelabrum, saved pictures that look
at us more than we look at them. We want death
or another type of dying. Want to take a breath
not our own, reorder nerves and chemistry
on a body-mind board game. Form a dynasty
for the self to inherit other bits and pieces
that fit chronology and need, different creases
of will and energy. The memory of roses
is more than she suspects. If she closes
a book, that book won't disappear—
that is, if she is willing, doesn't fear
the words will bury her alive,
the author not remember she once lived.

Merlin of the Harp
Dublin on August 17th at Dusk

As if his hair were woven by a vibration
as if his eyes had spilled into his fingers
to find the landscape for each tone
as if his ears had touched another sky
and brought it to a ground where
asphalt split and rippling waters ran
as if Grafton Street and fancy mannequins
in windows at his back
had waved themselves away
grateful to relinquish identity and claim
for the half-moon of his harp
for the dew-light of plucked strings
which caught the dark of sun-down
and tossed it back to day
as if there were no death
his bow a wand that played
lost spirits to new life
and children once lured by the piper
to the tunnel of their doom
are recalled this night to Dublin
when the harpist draws his elbow
spreading one hand like a palm frond
in the wind
to move across the strings
and on fingertips of sound
sets every found child free
and we know a stillness to our wandering
a strength to start again
as if we were inside the music
as if we had made it come

About the Author

Marilyn Jurich is Associate Professor of English at Suffolk University, Boston, where she teaches courses in Fantasy and Folklore, Speculative Literature, Children's Literature and Modern English Poetry. She has also taught Law and Literature and Verse Drama. An early work entitled *A Department Store Has Everything!..* (Todd Press, 1969), is a verse drama for children. Having been involved in children's theater during her late teens, she realized how very few original (and worthy) plays exist for children.

Many years later she realized another vacancy—how female characters in folktales had been "slighted." In 1998 in her book *Scheherazade's Sisters: Trickster Heroines and Their Stories in World Literature* (Greenwood Press), she established a new folklore type, the female trickster, called *trickstar*. In many ways distinct from the male trickster, *trickstar* generally improves the society she challenges.

While she has published many scholarly essays ranging from Dorothy Wordsworth's poetic imagination to Stanislaw Lem's science fiction novels and wrote the essay "Poetry for Children" in the *Oxford Encyclopedia of Children's Literature* (2006), she has always been writing poems. Her poems have appeared in journals such as *Ariel, Journal of the Fantastic in the Arts, Mid-stream, Tufts Review* and *Z*. Several of her poems have been anthologized, some have received honorary mention; in 1998 she was a winner of the "Anna Davidson Rosenberg Award for Poems on the Jewish Experience" and in 2003, she was one of the finalists for the Dana Award. Ottone Riccio, her teacher, in the "famous" poetry workshop at the Boston Center for Adult Education, has been a continual influence and inspiration.

Currently, she lives in Brookline, Massachusetts, with Joseph, her husband, recently retired from Framingham State University and a Mark Twain expert. Joscelyn, their daughter, adventures in New York where she teaches humanities, reviews books, and writes articles—often taking the photographs for these as well.

Other Recent Titles From Mayapple Press:

Jayne Pupek, *Forms of Intercession*, 2008
        Paper, 102 pp, $15.95 plus s&h
        ISBN 978-0932412-591
Elizabeth Kerlikowske, *Dominant Hand*, 2008
        Paper, 64 pp, $14.95 plus s&h
        ISBN 978-0932412-584
Patricia McNair, *Taking Notice*, 2007
        Paper, 60 pp, $14.95 plus s&h
        ISBN 978-0932412-560
James Owens, *Frost Lights a Thin Flame*, 2007
        Paper, 48 pp, $13.95 plus s&h
        ISBN 978-0932412-553
Chris Green, *The Sky Over Walgreens*, 2007
        Paper, 78 pp, $14.95 plus s&h
        ISBN 978-0932412-546
Mariela Griffor, *HOUSE*, 2007
        Paper, 50 pp, $14.95 plus s&h
        ISBN 978-0932412-539
John Repp, *Fever*, 2007
        Paper, 36 pp, $11.95 plus s&h
        ISBN 978-0932412-522
Kathryn Kirkpatrick, *Out of the Garden*, 2007
        Paper, 80 pp, $14.95 plus s&h
        ISBN 978-0932412-515
Gerry LaFemina, *The Book of Clown Baby/Figures from the Big Time Circus Book*, 2007
        Paper, 60 pp, $14.95 plus s&h
        ISBN 978-0932412-508
Nancy Botkin, *Parts That Were Once Whole*, 2007
        Paper, 72 pp, $14.95 plus s&h
        ISBN 978-0932412-492
David Lunde, *Instead,* 2007
        Paper, 72 pp, $14.95 plus s&h
        ISBN 978-0932412-485

For a complete catalog of Mayapple Press publications, please visit our website at *www.mayapplepress.com.* Books can be ordered direct from our website with secure on-line payment using PayPal, or by mail (check or money order).
Or order through your local bookseller.